Math for All Learners
Pre-Algebra

by

Pam Meader and Judy Storer

illustrated by Julie Mazur

J. WESTON
WALCH
PUBLISHER
Portland, Maine

User's Guide
to
Walch Reproducible Books

As part of our general effort to provide educational materials that are as practical and economical as possible, we have designated this publication a "reproducible book." The designation means that the purchase of the book includes purchase of the right to limited reproduction of all pages on which this symbol appears:

Here is the basic Walch policy: We grant to individual purchasers of this book the right to make sufficient copies of reproducible pages for use by all students of a single teacher. This permission is limited to a single teacher and does not apply to entire schools or school systems, so institutions purchasing the book should pass the permission on to a single teacher. Copying of the book or its parts for resale is prohibited.

Any questions regarding this policy or request to purchase further reproduction rights should be addressed to:

Permissions Editor
J. Weston Walch, Publisher
321 Valley Street • P.O. Box 658
Portland, Maine 04104-0658

1   2   3   4   5   6   7   8   9   10
ISBN 0-8251-3808-6
Copyright © 1998
J. Weston Walch, Publisher
P. O. Box 658 • Portland, Maine 04104-0658
Printed in the United States of America

Contents

To the Teacher

Since the early 1970's we have been teaching math to learners of all ages, from young children to adults, who represent many different cultures and socioeconomic backgrounds. We believe that all learners can do math by first overcoming any math anxiety and then participating in meaningful cooperative learning activities that foster the four major standards of Communication, Problem Solving, Connections, and Reasoning. These standards are founded in the Curriculum and Evaluation Standards for School Mathematics (1989), grades K–12. The draft of the content framework for *"Equipped for the Future" Standards for Adults* (1998) suggests that for adults to be "equipped for the future," they must be able to problem solve, make decisions, and communicate effectively using math concepts and technology in an ever-changing world.

Our goal is to encourage all learners to "know math by doing math." To this end, we have developed activities called "labs" that enable the learner to discover mathematical concepts through a hands-on approach. Cooperative learning skills are developed through group activities in which each learner participates collaboratively as a team member. Communication skills are fostered through group discussion and written reactions to lab discoveries. Many of the labs are connected to real-life situations. Other labs require learners to form generalizations about mathematical revelations.

As you look through the labs you will notice that many labs cluster around mathematical concepts of fractions, percents, geometry, and number relationships. Many of the labs require each group to report to the whole class. We suggest that teachers document these responses on the board or overhead for the whole class to see. This allows the students to look further at possible number patterns and relationships.

Probably the most important lab in our book is the lab entitled *Math Alphabet Soup*. In order for any of these labs to be successful, students should be made comfortable in the classroom. Many come with high levels of math anxiety and lack skills sufficient to work in groups. Beginning your course with the *Math Alphabet Soup* activity allows the students to vent their anxieties, realize they are not alone in their feelings, and begin to find ways to overcome this anxiety. It has been our experience that addressing math anxiety is very important in creating a classroom environment that will foster success.

Another suggestion we have is to begin journal writing in your math classroom. A journal could consist of some mathematical question the student must answer along with a reflection on their learning process. We have gained much knowledge about each of our students through their journal entries. Journals can be used as an alternative means of assessing whether a student *understands* a concept as well as checking the student's confidence level.

As teachers, we believe learning should be learner centered, not teacher driven. The response from our learners has been favorable. As one student said, "Thank you for turning my math disability into a math ability."

— Pam and Judy

Math Alphabet Soup

Learning Outcome

Students will be able to:

- communicate their feelings about math.
- develop math vocabulary.
- feel less anxious about math.

Overview

Students will write down the first word that comes to their mind about math for each letter of the alphabet. The words will then be discussed and rated in positive and negative terms.

Time

45–60 minutes

Team Size

Two to three students

Procedure

This is an excellent activity for the first class meeting, especially for students who have lots of math anxiety, feel they cannot do math, or do not like math. It will help you let students know that your job is to eliminate any math anxiety they have and prove to them that math is valuable in life and can be fun. We believe that only when math anxiety is decreased or preferably eliminated can real confidence and competence in math be developed. This can best be accomplished when math is presented in a multisensory way—a way that engages students in visual, auditory, kinesthetic, and tactile experiences.

1. Encourage students to write any words—either positive or negative—that enter their minds along with any math vocabulary that they might remember.

2. Make a class chart on the board or on an overhead, similar to the chart on page 3, with "Positive" on the left and "Negative" on the right.

3. List words from each team on the class chart.

4. Determine if the class as a whole rated their words more positive or more negative.

5. Encourage teams to discuss their words and their reasons for selecting them.

Through open discussion of the activity questions, students will begin to feel comfortable with their feelings about math and realize that if they do have negative feelings, they are shared with many. They will also realize that you accept and value their thoughts.

Name_____ Date _____

Math Alphabet Soup

Activity One

With your partner, brainstorm words that pop into your mind when you think of "math." Try to write two or three words for each letter of the alphabet.

A _____

B _____

C _____

D _____

E _____

F _____

G _____

H _____

I _____

J _____

K _____

L _____

M _____

N _____

O _____

P _____

Q _____

R _____

(continued)

Math Alphabet Soup *(continued)*

S _____

T _____

U _____

V _____

W _____

X _____

Y _____

Z _____

Now look at each word on your list. Decide whether the word is positive or negative. Write each word under the appropriate heading in the chart below.

Positive Words	Negative Words

(continued)

Math Alphabet Soup *(continued)*

Do you have more positive words or more negative words?

_____

If you could rate your positive words with a numerical value, what value would you give them? Why?

_____

_____

_____

_____

_____

If you could rate your negative words with a numerical value, what value would you give them? Why?

_____

_____

_____

_____

_____

Activity Two

Answer the following questions. Then share your answers with your partner(s).

    1. What math do you enjoy the most?

    _____

    _____

    _____

(continued)

Math Alphabet Soup *(continued)*

2. What math do you enjoy the least?

_____

_____

_____

3. Tell about a time when you really enjoyed doing math.

_____

_____

_____

4. Tell about a time when you had to use math outside school.

_____

_____

_____

5. In what jobs do you think people need to use math?

_____

_____

_____

Measuring in Mots, Prots, Stots, and Zots

Learning Outcome

Students will be able to:

- understand how measuring systems are organized.
- convert measures from one given unit to another.
- use estimation skills in determining measurement.

Overview

Students will develop a new measuring system and create a measuring tool using strips of paper.

Time

Two 45–60-minute periods

Team Size

Two students

Materials

Strips cut from 8½" × 11" sturdy white paper; markers; tape; scissors

Procedure

Activity One

1. It is important for students to take a moment to plan out the activity. Make sure that students **do not** use the English ruler as they begin to measure the mot (for teacher reference, the mot = 1 inch) and develop the other units of the Ot system.

2. As you circulate around the room, listen to the students' comments and offer suggestions if needed. Encourage students to use a pencil first as they section off their measuring stick in mots, prots, stots, and zots.

3. As students fill in the chart, stress the importance of estimating first. This skill will be necessary when they are introduced to the metric system.

Activity Two

1. As students begin developing their system, encourage discussion. Visit teams and have the students explain their system to you before they begin to construct their measuring stick.

2. Some problems may occur: Their measuring stick may become too large and unmanageable, or they may not correctly mark off their measuring stick in equal units of measure.

3. Depending on time, you may want to ask each team to explain its new measuring system.

Extensions

- Teams could measure with another team's measuring stick and compare systems.
- For further in-depth discovery, a team could research how measurement systems were designed.
- The teams could convert their units of measure to the English system and design a conversion chart for their system into English units. For example, in the Ot system, **1 mot = 1 inch**, etc.

Measuring in Mots, Prots, Stots, and Zots

Activity One

1. You and your partner are going to experiment measuring with a new measurement system, the Ot system of measure, being field-tested to replace the English system of measure. After trial tests, you will develop your own measuring system.

   To begin, you need to know that the following line measures one mot.

   ▬▬▬▬▬▬

   one mot

   You also need to know: **3 mots = 1 prot**

   3 prots = 1 stot

   3 stots = 1 zot

   Your task is to use strips of paper to make a measuring stick one **zot** long. Using the length of one mot as your guide, how do you and your partner plan to do this? Write your plan below.

   _____

   _____

   _____

2. Section off and label your new measuring stick in mots, prots, stots, and zots.

3. After you have constructed your new one-**zot** measuring stick, use it to measure the items in the chart on the next page. But first, **estimate** using the new units. Fill in the chart with your estimates and measurements.

(continued)

Measuring in Mots, Prots, Stots, and Zots *(continued)*

Object	Mots		Prots		Stots		Zots	
	Estim.	Actual	Estim.	Actual	Estim.	Actual	Estim.	Actual
length of your table								
height of door								
width of room								
your height								
your arm span								
length of your foot								
distance around your head								
length of your face from forehead to chin								

Activity Two

1. Now you and your partner are each going to create your own measuring system. Discuss how you might go about this and develop a plan. First, you need a unit of measure for your new system. Draw a line of any length and give it a nonsense name. Then write your table of equivalent measures on the back of this sheet.

    Draw your line here.

(continued)

Measuring in Mots, Prots, Stots, and Zots *(continued)*

2. Using strips of paper, create your new measuring stick by marking off the equivalent measures of your new system. Field-test your new system of measurement by completing the following chart. First estimate, then measure.

Unit of Measure								
Object	Estim.	Actual	Estim.	Actual	Estim.	Actual	Estim.	Actual
length of your table								
height of door								
width of room								
your height								
your arm span								
length of your foot								
distance around your head								
length of your face from forehead to chin								

3. Compare your new system with the Ot system. The mot is the smallest unit of measure in the Ot system. What is your smallest unit of measure? _____ How does your unit compare in size to the mot?_____

Inching Along the Ruler

Learning Outcome

Students will be able to:

- understand ½, ¼, ⅛, and ¹⁄₁₆ of an inch on a ruler.

- estimate to the nearest ½, ¼, ⅛, ¹⁄₁₆ of an inch on a ruler.

- feel more confident using the ruler as a measuring tool.

Overview

Students will demonstrate knowledge of ruler divisions by first dividing a line then folding a paper strip to check for accuracy.

Time

Two 45–60-minute periods

Team Size

Two students

Materials

Strips of paper 12" by 1" (five strips for each student); rulers; pencils; copies of templates 1 and 2; scissors

Procedure

Activity One

1. Have students begin by dividing the line with a pencil. This will allow you to quickly assess students' prior knowledge about fractions of an inch.

2. Next, have students fold a strip of paper into the appropriate divisions. This makes the concept of fractions of an inch more concrete.

3. Finally, allowing each team to demonstrate how they folded their strip while giving verbal instructions to the rest of the class reinforces the concept of part to whole. Stress the fact that one division on a ruler can have many names or represent equivalent fractions.

Activity Two

1. Make copies of the two templates on page 12 , and cut them apart.

2. Use template 1 to show the markings of the ruler as repeated divisions. First, cut the line into two equal pieces. The center line is the ½ line; stress that you have divided the line into two equal parts.

3. Next, divide the two half sections in half again. Stress that there are now four equal pieces, and each piece is ¼. Label each part ¼, ²⁄₄, ¾, ⁴⁄₄ so that students can see the fraction equivalents.

(continued)

10

4. Continue this pattern through sixteenths. With each new division, use a smaller mark, to resemble the markings on the ruler.

5. Some noticeable patterns are that 1 can be written with equal denominators and numerators, that equivelant fractions of ½ all have a numerator that is half the denominator, etc.

6. Template 2 includes ruler markings. This time, have students record the most efficient way to read the fractional markings. For instance, the lines representing ¼ and ¾ will be labeled, but the ½ mark will only be labeled ½ and not ²⁄₄. The markings for eighths that will be recorded are ⅛, ⅜, ⅝, and ⅞, becuase the other marks are included in ¼, ½, ¾, etc.

7. The number patterns students might notice is that the numerators are all odd and the denominators are all even. Also, for any marking, only the odd-numbered numerators will be marked—e.g. ⅛, ⅜, ⅝, ⅞.

8. When students have finished marking the divisions on Template 2, distribute a ruler to each group so that they can examine actual markings.

Extension

For another lesson, you may want to develop the decimal equivalent to the fractional parts of an inch. For example, ½ is the same as .50, or ½ of a dollar is 50¢. Relating the fractions to money is an easy way for students to grasp the decimal equivalent.

Inching Along the Ruler

Template 1

0   1

- Cut here

Template 2

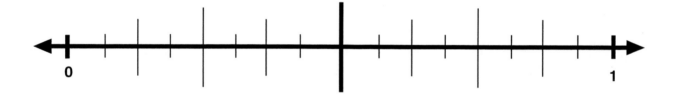

0   1

Inching Along the Ruler

Activity One

The line in Diagram 1 represents one inch on a ruler. Take a moment and think about how you would divide it into halves, fourths, eighths, and sixteenths. Show your divisions on the diagram.

Diagram 1

Share why you divided it in the way that you did by writing your thoughts here.

_____

_____

Compare your results with your partner's. Did you both divide the inch in the same way? Explain.

_____

_____

After sharing your thoughts, come to an agreement on how the inch should be divided. Demonstrate any changes on Diagram 2.

Diagram 2

To prove that your team is confident about its diagram, take a long strip of paper and fold it to resemble the divisions on your model inch diagram. When you and your team are finished, have one member demonstrate to the class how your team folded its strip. Pass out strips of paper for all of the teams so that they can follow your team member's directions.

After each team has demonstrated and each class member has experienced all strategies, determine whether you want to change the divisions on your model inch. Make the new divisions on this model inch diagram or recopy your first one.

Diagram 3

(continued)

Inching Along the Ruler *(continued)*

Activity Two

Template 1 represents an enlarged version of an inch with no divisions. Take template 1 and follow your teacher's directions to divide the inch using the markings that you would find on a ruler. Look at the divisions. Discuss with your partner(s) any number patterns that appear. Describe these patterns below.

_____

_____

What do you notice about the division marks?

_____

_____

_____

As each mark gets shorter, the value of the fraction gets smaller as well. Label the marks below with the correct fraction equivalent.

_____ inch mark _____ inch mark _____ inch mark _____ inch mark

The teacher will pass out an enlarged version of inch (template 2) with these divison marks on it. Label each division mark. Compare your labeling with your partner(s). Do you agree?

_____

Do you notice any number patterns with the way you have labeled the inch? Explain.

_____

The teacher will now pass out a ruler. What do you notice about the ruler?

_____

Locate the ½ inch, ¼ inch, ⅛ inch, and ¹⁄₁₆ inch markings.

Rim Around the Shape

Learning Outcome

Students will be able to:

- describe polygons (square, rectangle, triangle, parallelogram, irregular shape) and their characteristics.
- develop perimeter formulas from repeated patterns.

Overview

Students will work with cut-out shapes to discover perimeter formulas.

Time

45–60 minutes

Team Size

Three to four students

Materials

Cut-out cardboard squares, rectangles, parallelograms, triangles, and irregular shapes of various sizes (one of which has at least five noncongruent sides); string; rulers; optional: calculators with fraction key

Procedure

1. Begin this activity by having students name the shapes they can see in the classroom. This lets you assess what students already know about the various shapes and their names.

2. Next, begin a class discussion of the names of the figures and their various characteristics.

3. Distribute a set of cardboard shapes to each group. If you use the shapes in the template on page 89, enlarge them in varying percents on a photocopier. It is important for each group to have the same shapes, but in different sizes.

4. Have students compare the size of each shape to its perimeter through estimation.

5. Before beginning the next task, the class may need to review how to read and measure with an English ruler. This task gives the students practice measuring and sensing what perimeter means, i.e., "the distance around."

6. Problems may arise in adding fractions of unlike denominators. This activity could be modified to have the class measure to the nearest whole, ½, or ¼ inch, or to measure in centimeters so that students would be dealing only with decimals. Alternatively, students could use a calculator with a fraction key.

7. After all teams have recorded their measurements, create a class chart on the board or overhead to record each group's dimensions for each shape. One student from each team will post the team's findings on the class chart.

(continued)

8. Once all teams have reported, allow time for teammates to discuss what patterns they observe before opening the discussion up to the entire class.

9. Once the discussions are complete, ask students to find generalizations for determining the perimeter of each shape. Students should derive the perimeter formulas based on the patterns they observe in the given data.

   Example: For the square, students may generalize and say "side + side + side + side." Ask what would be a quicker way. The response is usually "four times a side." From the generalization, the algebraic way would be $4 \times s$ or $4s$.

10. The last part of the activity prompts students to assign the word "formula" to the generalizations they have developed.

Rim Around the Shape

1. Look around the room and list as many different shapes as you can.

   _____

   _____

   _____

   _____

2. You will be given five cardboard shapes. First, examine each shape and determine its name. Next, estimate the distance around each shape. Order the shapes according to the size of their boundaries from the smallest to the largest. Using that order, write the names of the shapes in the blanks below.

1._____ 2._____ 3._____ 4._____ 5._____

3. Using the chart below, fill in the names of your shapes and your estimates of their boundaries.

Shape	Estimate

(continued)

Rim Around the Shape *(continued)*

4. Measure each side of each shape. Record the dimensions (measures of each side) under the correct headings in the chart below. Make sure all team members agree on the results. Designate someone from your team to post your findings on the class chart.

	Side 1	Side 2	Side 3	Side 4	Side 5	Total (sum of all sides)
Square						
Rectangle						
Parallelogram						
Triangle						
Irregular shape						

Discuss with your team any patterns that you observe for each shape. Record your findings below.

Square _____

Rectangle _____

Parallelogram _____

Triangle _____

Irregular shape _____

(continued)

Rim Around the Shape (continued)

5. Can you now determine a generalization or a way to figure out the distance around each shape regardless of size?

Shape	Generalization
Square	
Rectangle	
Parallelogram	
Triangle	
Irregular shape	

Be ready to share your generalizations with the class. After hearing the generalizations of other teams, would you change your generalization? If so, how?

_____

_____

_____

What is another name for a generalization that you may hear more commonly in math class?

_____

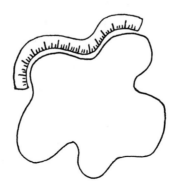

Greatest vs. Smallest PeRIMeter

Learning Outcome

Students will be able to:

- use estimation skills to determine perimeter.
- calculate perimeters of various shapes (square, rectangle, triangle, parallelogram, and irregular shapes).
- maximize and minimize perimeters.

Overview

Students will use five shapes (triangle, square, rectangle, parallelogram, and irregular figure) to create a design with the largest and then the smallest possible perimeter.

Time

Two 45–60-minute periods

Team Size

Two students

Materials

Two sets of shapes copied from page 89 for each team (if possible, copied onto oaktag or heavy paper); calculators (fraction key desirable); rulers; 18" x 36" construction paper; glue. Colored pencils, markers, or crayons are optional.

Procedure

1. Instruct teams to determine the dimensions and perimeters by estimating. You should specify whether you want them to measure in inches or centimeters. Measuring in centimeters will minimize the need to measure in fractional units.

2. Encourage them to lay their shapes out on the construction paper and number them according to their perimeters before they log their results on the chart. Each teammate should measure all shapes and agree on the calculations before recording them on the chart.

3. If students have difficulty measuring fractional units with a ruler, instruct them to measure to the nearest whole inch, ½ inch, ¼ inch, etc.

4. You may want to encourage students to write the dimensions on the shapes in pencil.

5. In the next part of the activity, students are asked to create shapes with the greatest and smallest possible perimeter. The only rule is that one side of each shape must completely touch one side of another shape. Model this process for students.

6. Have each team share its creations with the entire class. Allow time to observe each team's designs to determine what characteristics determine greatest vs. smallest perimeter.

Extension

Ask all students to figure the area of each of their classmates' designs to see who had the greatest area and the smallest area.

Greatest vs. Smallest PeRIMeter

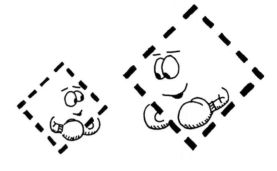

1. You have been given five shapes (square, rectangle, triangle, parallelogram, and irregular shape).

2. Estimate the dimensions (length of each side) of each shape. Record your estimates on the chart on the next page.

3. Arrange the five shapes from the smallest perimeter to the greatest perimeter.

4. Estimate the perimeter of each shape. Record your estimates on the chart on the next page.

5. Now, let's see what good estimators you and your partner were. Using a ruler, determine the exact perimeter of each shape by measuring its sides (dimensions).

6. Record the dimensions and perimeter on the chart on the next page.

(continued)

Greatest vs. Smallest PeRIMeter *(continued)*

Shape	Estimated Dimensions	Exact Dimenstions	Estimated Perimeter	Exact Perimeter
Square				
Rectangle				
Triangle				
Parallelogram				
Irregular Shape				

Greatest Perimeter

7. First, you and your partner will create a design using the five shapes you have been given. The object is to make the greatest perimeter you can. The only rule is that one complete side of one shape must completely touch a side of another shape. Your teacher will model this for you.

8. When you have figured the positioning of your shapes, glue them down on a large piece of paper. You may color your design and record its perimeter in the upper right-hand corner under your names.

(continued)

Greatest vs. Smallest PeRIMeter *(continued)*

Smallest Perimeter

9. Your second task is to take a second set of the same five shapes and figure out a design using all five shapes that has the smallest perimeter. Again, the only rule is that one complete side of each shape must completely touch a side of another shape.

10. When both designs are complete, share them with the class to see who designed the shapes with the greatest and smallest perimeters.

11. Observe each team's designs and write down characteristics that seem to make certain designs have greater or smaller perimeters.

I think the reasons for the greatest perimeters are _____

_____

_____

_____

I think the reasons for the smallest perimeters are _____

_____

_____

_____

_____

Developing Area Formulas

Learning Outcome

Students will be able to:

- develop the formulas for the areas of a rectangle and parallelogram.
- identify length and width or base and height.
- understand the concept of area as square units.

Overview

Students will work with cutout rectangles and parallelograms to discover area formulas.

Time

20 minutes

Team Size

Two to three students

Materials

Centimeter square grid paper (copied from page 90); cut-out parallelograms of various sizes, with heights noted (page 28); scissors; tape

---

Procedure

In this activity, students are introduced to the concept of area as a covering of square units. By finding a shortcut to counting the squares in the rectangle, students will derive and understand the formula for the area of a rectangle.

Area of a Rectangle

1. Distribute centimeter square grid paper (copied from page 90), scissors, and tape to each group. Students will cut a rectangle from the grid paper, then determine its length, width, and area by counting the number of squares.

2. Encourage students to see that the relationship between the area of the rectangle and its length and width is that the length multiplied by the width equals the area.

3. Students should translate their findings into the formula $A = l \bullet w$. Some students may need help moving from the statement of their findings to the generalization of a formula.

Area of a Parallelogram

4. Give each student a cutout parallelogram with the height drawn, page 28. Students should label the base and height of the parallelogram b and h.

(continued)

5. Students cut the parallelogram along its height to form two figures. They then rearrange the two shapes to form a rectangle, as shown below, and tape the rectangle to their handouts.

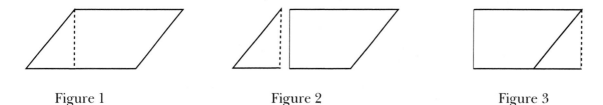

Figure 1   Figure 2   Figure 3

6. Students label the length and width of the rectangle. They should recognize that the length and width of the rectangle are the same as the height and base of the parallelogram.

7. Encourage students to see that they can use the formula they derived for the area of a rectangle to find the area of the parallelogram. Since they formed the rectangle from the parallelogram, they should recognize that the area of the parallelogram will be the same as the area of the rectangle. If necessary, suggest that students count the number of squares in both shapes to see that they are the same.

8. Since students have determined that the base and height of the parallelogram are the same as the length and width of the rectangle, they should derive the formula for the area of a parallelogram, A = b • h.

Developing Area Formulas

In these two activities, you will determine the formulas for the area of a rectangle and of a parallelogram.

Activity One: Area of a Rectangle

The area of any figure is the number of **square units** it contains.

Take a piece of centimeter square grid paper and cut out a rectangle that can fit in the space below. Tape it in place. Label the length and width.

1. How many units long is the rectangle? _____

2. How many units wide is the rectangle? _____

3. How many square units are in the whole surface? _____

4. What relation do you see between the length, width, and area of a rectangle?

_____

5. Write the formula here for finding the area of a rectangle.

_____

(continued)

Developing Area Formulas *(continued)*

Activity Two: Area of a Parallelogram

You and your partner(s) will each be given a parallelogram. Note the dotted perpendicular line on the parallelogram. This is called the **height** of the parallelogram. The **base** of the parallelogram is the side that the **height** is drawn perpendicular to. Label the base *b* and the height *h* on your parallelogram. Carefully separate the parallelogram into two pieces by cutting along the height. Rearrange the two pieces, to form a rectangle. Tape the newly formed rectangle below. Then *outside* the rectangle, label the length *l* and the width *w*.

1. What do you observe about the base and height of the parallelogram and the length and width of the rectangle?

   _____

   _____

2. How can you find the area of the rectangle you have just formed?

   _____

3. Will the area of this rectangle be the same as the area of the parallelogram? Why or why not?

   _____

4. What do you think might be a formula for finding the area of a parallelogram? Write your formula below.

   _____

(continued)

Developing Area Formulas *(continued)*

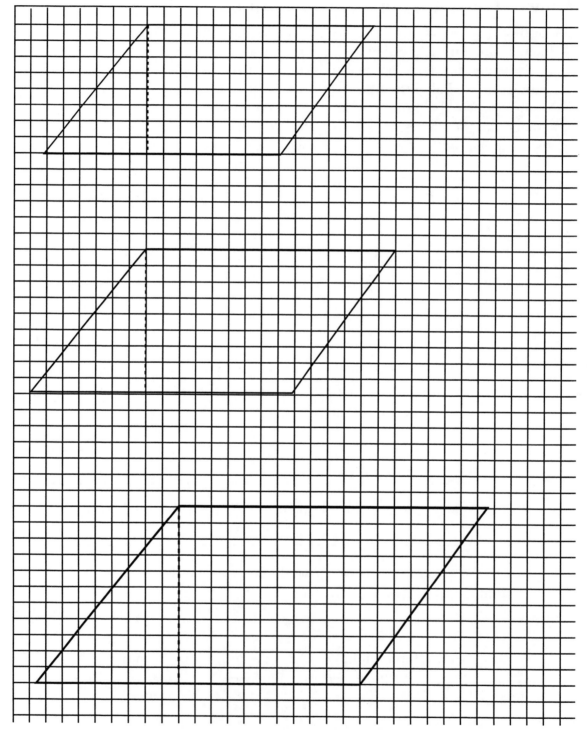

Area of a Triangle

Learning Outcome

Students will be able to:

• discover the relationship between the area of a rectangle and the area of a triangle.

• understand why the area of a triangle is half that of a rectangle.

Overview

Students will work with cutout triangles to discover the formula for the area of a triangle.

Time

20–30 minutes

Team Size

Two students

Materials

Paper rectangles cut into three triangles (page 31); rulers

Procedure

This activity works well as a continuation of the previous activity, Developing Area Formulas. Students should know how to find the area of a rectangle before doing this activity.

1. Make enough copies of the rectangle on page 31 for each group. Cut the copies apart to form three triangles. Distribute a set of the triangles to each group.

2. Teams work together to form the three triangles into the original rectangle. They should then measure the length and width of the rectangle, and determine its area.

3. Next, students form the three triangles into two identical triangles, as shown below. If students are having difficulty with this, suggest that the two smaller triangles will exactly fit into the larger triangle.

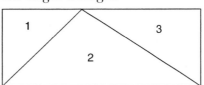

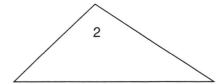 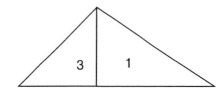

(continued)

4. Some students may have difficulty seeing that the total area of the two identical triangles is the same as the area of the original rectangle. If necessary, remind students that they haven't reduced the area of the rectangle, they have just rearranged it.

5. Because it takes the area of two identical triangles to make the area of one rectangle and the area of a rectangle is $l \cdot w$ or $b \cdot h$, it follows that the area of one triangle must be half of the area of a rectangle: $A = \frac{1}{2} bh$.

Area of a Triangle

Make copies of this page. Cut apart to form sets of three triangles.

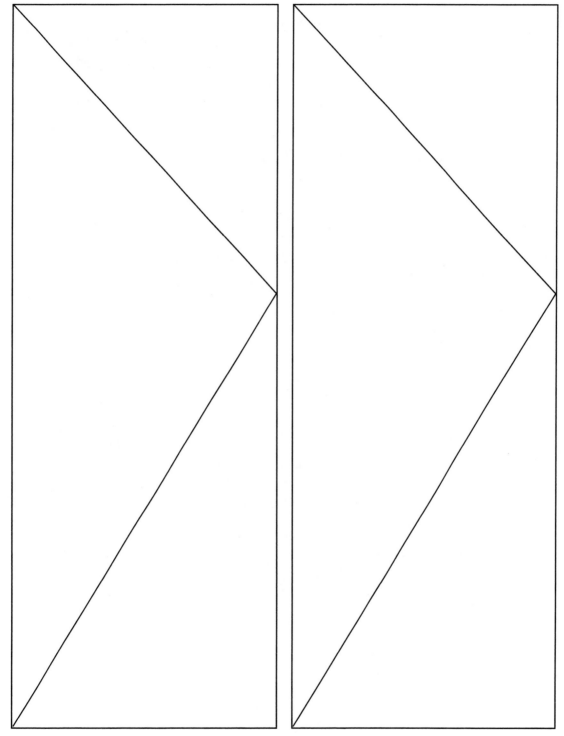

(continued)

Area of a Triangle *(continued)*

You will be given three triangular shapes. Try to place the three pieces together to form a rectangle. (It may take a few tries, but it can be done.)

 Once you have formed the rectangle, measure its length and width to the nearest centimeter and record below:

Length _____ Width _____

What is the area of the rectangle? _____

Now, with the three shapes, see if you can form two identical triangles. (Again, it may take a few tries, but two identical triangles can be formed.)

What is the *total* area of the two triangles? _____

How could you determine the area of one of the triangles? _____

_____

The two identical triangles you formed were originally the rectangle you described above. The area of a rectangle is *lw* (length times width), which is the same as, *bh* (base times height). Using *bh* (base times height), can you determine a formula for finding the area of one triangle? Write the formula here:

_____

Floor Plan with
Constant PeRIMeter

Learning Outcome

Students will be able to:

- discriminate between perimeter and area.
- communicate, through reasoning and problem solving, factors that affect area.

Overview

Using centimeter square paper, students will draw and cut out three floor plans using the same perimeter.

Time

One or two 45-minute periods

Team Size

Three to four students

Materials

Centimeter grid paper (page 90—enough for each person to have at least two sheets); scissors; clear tape; 18" × 36" light-colored construction paper (one piece per team); black markers; transparency of centimeter grid

Procedure

1. Using a centimeter grid transparency copied from page 90, model for the class how to draw a shape and stay on the lines.
2. Ask students to name a shape with a perimeter of 36 cm that they could easily draw. Responses will include a square and a rectangle.
3. Then ask what the dimensions of a rectangle or square would have to be to get a perimeter of 36 cm (12 × 6, 15 × 3, 9 × 9). Draw a rectangle to illustrate.
4. Draw an irregular shape to show them they must stay on the lines. Demonstrate that they cannot draw a diagonal line through any square centimeter.
5. Encourage students to draw at least two irregular shapes. Many students will be able to draw the irregular shapes, but others will have difficulty. Check an irregular shape of at least one member of each team to ensure that at least one member is able to do the task. Encourage those who find it easy to offer suggestions and model their method for others on their team.
6. When all shapes are cut, ordered, and taped, have each team title its chart, write each team member's name on the chart, and write their key findings in black marker.
7. Have all team representatives share their findings with the entire class, and then ask the class to summarize key points. Many findings will be the same concepts expressed differently. Look for these findings:
   • The square shape has the greatest area.
   • As irregular shapes approach square shapes, their areas become greater.
   • The more cuts or sides or angles a shape has, the smaller the area.
   • The more elongated or stretched out or skinny a shape is, the smaller the area.
   • The more compact a shape is, the greater the area.

Floor Plan with Constant PeRIMeter

Your team members have each been asked to draw three floor plans for a contractor who is building new homes in your area. Your floor plans must meet the following criteria:

(a) Each floor plan must have a perimeter of exactly 36 cm.

(b) The contractor is looking for unusual plans, so make sure at least one plan is not rectangular.

(c) When you draw your floor plans, you **must** stay on the lines. **Do not** draw through a square centimeter.

Draw your floor plans on centimeter grid paper. Each team member must prepare three plans. Have a team member double-check to make sure your plans meet all the above criteria. Then cut out your floor plans and complete the following activities.

1. Count the total number of square centimeters (area) of each of your floor plans and write the total on each plan.

2. Order your floor plans according to area, from the smallest to the largest.

3. Compare your floor plans with your partners'. Order **all** of them from smallest to largest areas. Then tape all the plans on a piece of construction paper. This will be your team's chart.

4. Examine the team chart. Write on the lines below at least three discoveries you have made during this activity.

_____

_____

_____

(continued)

Floor Plan with Constant PeRIMeter *(continued)*

5. Share your discoveries with your team members. Have one team member record a summary of your group's discoveries on your team's chart.

6. Nominate a spokesperson to share your team's findings with the rest of the class.

After each team shares its findings with the entire class, answer the following questions:

1. What was your smallest area? _____

   What was your team's smallest area? _____

   What was the class's smallest area? _____

2. Do you think that the smallest possible area has been found? _____

   _____

   If not, how small could the area be with a perimeter of 36 cm? _____

3. What happens to the figure when the area becomes smaller? _____

   _____

   _____

4. What was your largest area? _____

   What was your team's largest area? _____

   What was the class's largest area? _____

5. Do you think that the largest possible area has been found? _____

   _____

   If not, how large could the area be with a perimeter of 36 cm? _____

   _____

6. What shape appears to give the largest area?

   _____

The Largest vs. the Smallest Sneaker

Learning Outcome

Students will be able to:

- differentiate between perimeter and area.
- use the formulas for perimeter and area of a rectangle.
- recognize the fact that equal perimeters do not always imply equal areas.

Overview

Students will trace their sneaker or shoe on centimeter grid paper and compare the area and perimeter of their shoe size to others in the class.

Time

45–60 minutes

Team Size

Two students

Materials

Centimeter grid paper (page 90—two sheets per student); string; centimeter ruler; tape

Procedure

1. Pass out centimeter grid paper copied from page 90. Some students will need to tape two sheets together (to accommodate large sneakers). If students are not wearing sneakers, reassure them that the lab works perfectly well with shoes.

2. Make sure that the students read through the directions first and ask questions before attempting the activity.

3. If a student cannot find someone (a "sneaker partner") with the same perimeter, let him or her find the closest perimeter.

4. Some students may confuse the perimeter and area formulas for a rectangle. If needed, review the formulas:

   $P = 2l + 2w$ or $P = 2(l + w)$

   $A = lw$

Extension

Discuss how the size of boys' sneakers compares to that of girls' sneakers (boys' tend to be wider and two sizes larger than girls').

Name_____ Date _____

The Largest vs. the Smallest Sneaker

1. Trace your right sneaker (or shoe) as precisely as possible on centimeter grid paper. Estimate the number of square centimeters contained within the perimeter of your sneaker. Record here:

   _____

2. Find the perimeter of your sneaker by taking a piece of string and wrapping it around the outer sole of the sneaker. Measure the length of the string in centimeters. Record here:

   _____

3. Find a "sneaker partner" who has the same or about the same length string for their estimated sneaker perimeter as you. Record both perimeters and estimated sneaker areas.

   Your perimeter _____ Sneaker partner's perimeter _____

   Your area _____ Sneaker partner's area _____

   Are your sneaker areas about the same? _____

   If you answered no, why do you think the areas are different when your perimeters are about the same?

   _____

   _____

   _____

   _____

4. Use ruler to draw the smallest rectangle you can around the tracing of your sneaker on the centimeter grid paper.

   Record the dimensions of your rectangle. _____

   What's the perimeter of your rectangle in centimeters? _____

(continued)

The Largest vs. the Smallest Sneaker (continued)

5. What is the area of your rectangle in square centimeters? _____

   Compare the dimensions of your rectangle with your partner's rectangle:

   Your dimensions _____   Partner's dimensions _____

6. Compare the perimeter of your rectangle with your partner's rectangle:

   Your perimeter _____   Partner's perimeter _____

   Compare the area of your rectangle with your partner's rectangle:

   Your area _____   Partner's area _____

7. In summary, does the same length perimeter mean you have the same size sneaker? _____

   Does having the same sneaker areas determine that you have the same sizes? _____

   Do both the area and perimeter of your sneakers need to be the same to determine size? _____

   Explain._____

   _____

   _____

   _____

   _____

   _____

Fraction Circles

Learning Outcome

Students will be able to:

- understand a fraction as part to a whole amount.
- determine which fraction is larger, both visually and mathematically.
- determine equivalent fractions, both visually and mathematically.
- estimate whether a fraction is close to 0, close to ½, or close to 1.

Overview

Using fraction circle manipulatives, students will discover relationships of size, ordering, and estimation of common fractions.

Time

30–40 minutes

Team Size

Two students

Materials

Commercial fraction circles

Procedure

1. The first part of the activity lets students become familiar with the fraction circle manipulatives. They should observe that the fraction pieces are different colors for the different shapes. They may observe that the different shapes decrease in size. Some may find parts that fit on top of other parts. For example, two ¼ pieces fit exactly on a ½ piece.

2. Next, students group the fraction circles by color, and determine which fraction of a circle each color represents. Answers will vary depending on the set of fraction circles you have.

3. The next part of the activity asks students to take one piece of each color, arrange them according to size, and write the fraction each piece represents. Students should see that, as the denominator gets larger, the fraction gets smaller.

4. Have students take five pieces of each color and arrange them (by color) in partial circles, from most complete circle to least complete circle. They should notice that, provided the numerator stays the same, the circle fills up more slowly as the denominator gets larger.

5. To reinforce this concept, students are asked to select the larger fraction from three similar pairs. a) 8/17 b) 8/12 c) 3/5

6. In this step, students are asked to find fraction pieces that are close to but less than ½, and list them in relation to ½, using <. They should notice that fractions that are close to ½ have denominatiors that are almost double the numerators.

7. This time, students are asked to find fractions that are close to 1. They should notice that fractions that are close to 1 have numerators and denominators that are nearly equal.

Fraction Circles

1. Spread out the fraction circle pieces on a desk. With your partner, examine the pieces and write your observations below.

_____

_____

_____

_____

_____

_____

2. Group the pieces by color. Determine what fraction of a whole circle each color represents.

Green _____   Blue _____

Red _____   Orange _____

Purple _____   Yellow _____

3. Take one piece of each color. Arrange them according to size from the largest to the smallest piece. Write the value of each piece on the lines below.

_____ _____ _____ _____ _____ _____ _____

Largest piece   Smallest piece

As the numerator stays the same and the denominator gets larger, what happens to the size of the fraction? _____

_____

4. Take five pieces from each of the following groups: ⅙, ⅛, ⅒, ¹⁄₁₂. Use the five ⅙ pieces to form a partial circle. Do the same with the pieces in the other three colors. You should have four partial circles, each a different color. Arrange your partial circles according to completeness of the circle, from largest part of a

(continued)

Fraction Circles (continued)

circle to smallest part of a circle. Write the fraction value represented by each partial circle below.

_____   _____

Largest   Smallest

As the numerator stays the same and the denominator gets larger, what happens to the size of the fraction?

5. From what you have discovered, circle the larger fraction in each pair below.

   a) 8/17 8/21   b) 7/12 7/12   c) 3/5 3/10

6. Take the ½ circle. Use pieces of other colors to find fractions that are close to but less than ½. List the fractions below.

   Example: ⅖ < ½

   _____   _____   _____

   _____   _____   _____

   _____   _____   _____

   _____   _____   _____

   What observations can you make about fractions that are close to ½?

   _____

7. Using the fraction pieces, find fractions that are close to but less than 1. List them below.

   _____

   What observations can you make about fractions that are close to 1?

   _____

Fraction to Decimal Patterns

Learning Outcome

Students will be able to:

- recognize and explain number patterns that occur when changing fractions into decimals.

- identify some fraction/decimal equivalents.

Overview

Using a calculator, students will discover interesting patterns with repeating decimals.

Time

45–60 minutes

Team Size

Two students

Materials

Calculators

Procedure

1. Distribute work sheets and have teams work through the first two sets of fractions. As students are entering the fractions into the calculator, check that they are entering the values in the correct order—that is, numerator divided by denominator.

2. Once the activity is complete, open up student discoveries for class discussion.

3. When discussion has ceased, have the students do the remaining fractions.

4. Many of these fractions have interesting patterns. The sevenths always have a 6-digit repetend whose order keeps changing. For instance, $\frac{1}{7}$ is .142857, and $\frac{2}{7}$ begins with .285714 (note how the 14 moves to the back). This keeps happening for each of the sevenths (see figure 1).
   The ninths are also interesting; the repetend is whatever the numerator is—that is, $\frac{1}{9}$ is .1111$\overline{1}$, $\frac{2}{9}$ is .2222$\overline{2}$, etc. The elevenths also create interesting decimals. The repetends are multiples of 9. For instance, $\frac{1}{11} = 0.0909\overline{09}$, while $\frac{2}{11} = .1818\overline{18}$ (2×9), $\frac{3}{11} = .2727\overline{27}$ (3×9), etc.

Extensions

- Have students perform the same operations on fractions with denominators of 0, 1, 4, 5, 6, 8, 10, and 12, then answer these questions:

Which decimals are halves or doubles of each other?

Which fractions have decimals that looked like amounts of money?

What happens when you divide zero by any number other than zero?

(continued)

Figure 1. **Answer Key**

Fraction/decimal equivalences

Num	0	1	2	3	4	5	6	7	8	9	10	11	12
denom	0												
2	0	0.5	1	1.5	2	2.5	3	3.5	4	4.5	5	5.5	6
3	0	.33333̄	.66666̄	1	1.33333̄	1.66666̄	2	2.33333̄	2.66666̄	3	3.33333̄	3.66666̄	4
7	0	.142857	.285714	.428571	.571428	.714285	.857142	1	1.142857	1.285714	1.428571	1.571428	1.857142
9	0	.111̄	.2222̄	.33333̄	.4444̄	.5555̄	.666666̄	.77777̄	.88888̄	1	1.111̄	1.22222̄	1.33333̄
11	0	.090909̄	.181818̄	.272727̄	.363636̄	.454545̄	.545454̄	.63636363̄	.72727272̄	.81818181̄	.90909090̄	1	1.090909̄

Fraction to Decimal Patterns

With your partner, enter each fraction below into your calculator like a division problem. For example, ½ would be entered into the calculator as 1 ÷ 2 = . Record the decimal equivalents. Then discuss any patterns that you notice.

$\frac{0}{2}=$ _____ $\frac{1}{2}=$ _____ $\frac{2}{2}=$ _____ $\frac{3}{2}=$ _____ $\frac{4}{2}=$ _____

$\frac{5}{2}=$ _____ $\frac{6}{2}=$ _____ $\frac{7}{2}=$ _____ $\frac{8}{2}=$ _____

$\frac{9}{2}=$ _____ $\frac{10}{2}=$ _____ $\frac{11}{2}=$ _____ $\frac{12}{2}=$ _____

What pattern(s) do you notice with these fractions? _____

_____

Based on your discovery, state at least one rule that you think would work for changing any fraction that has a denominator of two into its decimal equivalent.

_____

_____

(continued)

Fraction to Decimal Patterns (continued)

$$\frac{0}{3} = \underline{\hspace{1.5cm}} \qquad \frac{1}{3} = \underline{\hspace{1.5cm}} \qquad \frac{2}{3} = \underline{\hspace{1.5cm}} \qquad \frac{3}{3} = \underline{\hspace{1.5cm}} \qquad \frac{4}{3} = \underline{\hspace{1.5cm}}$$

$$\frac{5}{3} = \underline{\hspace{1.5cm}} \qquad \frac{6}{3} = \underline{\hspace{1.5cm}} \qquad \frac{7}{3} = \underline{\hspace{1.5cm}} \qquad \frac{8}{3} = \underline{\hspace{1.5cm}}$$

$$\frac{9}{3} = \underline{\hspace{1.5cm}} \qquad \frac{10}{3} = \underline{\hspace{1.5cm}} \qquad \frac{11}{3} = \underline{\hspace{1.5cm}} \qquad \frac{12}{3} = \underline{\hspace{1.5cm}}$$

What pattern(s) do you notice with these fractions? _____

_____

Based on your discovery, state at least one rule that you think would work for changing any fraction that has a denominator of 3 into its decimal equivalant.

_____

_____

Change the following fractions to decimals as you did on the previous page.

$$\frac{0}{7} = \underline{\hspace{1.5cm}} \qquad \frac{1}{7} = \underline{\hspace{1.5cm}} \qquad \frac{2}{7} = \underline{\hspace{1.5cm}} \qquad \frac{3}{7} = \underline{\hspace{1.5cm}} \qquad \frac{4}{7} = \underline{\hspace{1.5cm}}$$

$$\frac{5}{7} = \underline{\hspace{1.5cm}} \qquad \frac{6}{7} = \underline{\hspace{1.5cm}} \qquad \frac{7}{7} = \underline{\hspace{1.5cm}} \qquad \frac{8}{7} = \underline{\hspace{1.5cm}}$$

$$\frac{9}{7} = \underline{\hspace{1.5cm}} \qquad \frac{10}{7} = \underline{\hspace{1.5cm}} \qquad \frac{11}{7} = \underline{\hspace{1.5cm}} \qquad \frac{12}{7} = \underline{\hspace{1.5cm}}$$

The sevenths are an interesting group of fractions. What discoveries did you make about changing sevenths to decimals?

_____

_____

(continued)

Fraction to Decimal Patterns (continued)

The ninths and the thirds have a pattern in common. Can you guess what the decimal equivalents will be for the ninths before you enter them in the calculator?

_____

_____

Now use your calculator.

$\frac{0}{9} =$ _____ $\frac{1}{9} =$ _____ $\frac{2}{9} =$ _____ $\frac{3}{9} =$ _____ $\frac{4}{9} =$ _____

$\frac{5}{9} =$ _____ $\frac{6}{9} =$ _____ $\frac{7}{9} =$ _____ $\frac{8}{9} =$ _____

$\frac{9}{9} =$ _____ $\frac{10}{9} =$ _____ $\frac{11}{9} =$ _____ $\frac{12}{9} =$ _____

Were your guesses correct? _____

What rule can you state for changing ninths into decimal equivalents?

_____

_____

The elevenths also are interesting decimals. Complete the following and see what happens.

$\frac{0}{11} =$ _____ $\frac{1}{11} =$ _____ $\frac{2}{11} =$ _____ $\frac{3}{11} =$ _____ $\frac{4}{11} =$ _____

$\frac{5}{11} =$ _____ $\frac{6}{11} =$ _____ $\frac{7}{11} =$ _____ $\frac{8}{11} =$ _____

$\frac{9}{11} =$ _____ $\frac{10}{11} =$ _____ $\frac{11}{11} =$ _____ $\frac{12}{11} =$ _____

What did you find? _____

Human Ratios

Learning Outcome

Students will be able to:

- determine equivalent ratios.

- represent comparisons as a ratio.

- express a ratio in a variety of ways.

- understand the concept of constant ratio.

- understand the effect of order in a ratio.

Overview

Students will discover various constant body ratios through measurement.

Time

45–60 minutes

Team Size

Two students

Materials

String, enough for students to measure height; measuring devices (rulers, yardsticks, tape measures); scissors; calculators

Procedure

1. Place spools of string, measuring devices, and scissors on a table for students to access.

2. As students explore their ratios, make sure they understand that a ratio of 1 to 3 is not the same as a ratio of 3 to 1. A review of changing a ratio to a decimal may be needed before they attempt problem 4.

3. Problems 4–8 reinforce the concept of constant ratio. On the board or an overhead, make a chart to record the results from problem 4. Include the following columns: height: head; head: height. Have students record their height-to-head decimal ratios on the chart.

4. Discuss what conclusions they made. Here is where you can emphasize that order in a ratio is important.

5. Let the students come up with their own definition of constant ratio in problem 5 and then determine with the class the best definitions of constant ratio.

6. Have students continue with problems 6–8 for further practice.

Extension

Paleontologists use the idea of constant ratio for constructing dinosaur models. Have students research what parts of the dinosaur are used to determine height, etc.

Human Ratios

1. First, cut a piece of string you estimate would represent your partner's height. Next, actually measure your partner's height with your string to see how close you were. Measure your string with a yardstick and compare it to the actual height of your partner. Now, ask your partner to perform the same steps. How close were your estimates?

_____

2. Next, cut a piece of string the exact height of your partner and estimate how many times you could wrap that string around your partner's head.

   Your guess is: _____

   Your partner will do the same. His or her guess is: _____

3. Now take the strings representing the actual heights and wrap them around your heads.

   What did you discover?

   _____

   How could you write this as a ratio?

   _____

   Were your ratio and your partner's ratio about the same?

   _____

   Is there more than one way that you can express this as a ratio?

   _____

   Record other ways here.

   _____

(continued)

Human Ratios *(continued)*

4. Express your height in inches. Measure the distance around your head in inches. Find the ratio of your height to your head. _____

_____

Find the ratio of your head to your height. _____

_____

Change these ratios to decimals by entering the ratios into your calculator and compare this result to your ratios in number 3. Are any about the same?

_____

Record your decimal ratio on the class chart. Once all students have reported their decimal ratios, what conclusion can you draw about the ratio of height to the distance around your head?

_____

5. The ratio that you have discovered is an example of a constant ratio. What do you think a **constant ratio** is?

_____

_____

6. If someone's height is 57", what should be the distance around his or her head?

_____

7. If someone's head measures 23", how tall should this person be?

_____

8. Prove which of the following are also constant ratios:
   a. Height to your foot measurement
   b. Height to hand-span measurement
   c. Height to arm-span measurement
   d. Height to forearm measurement

Circumference of Cookies and Cost Comparison

Learning Outcome

Students will be able to:

- identify radius, diameter, and circumference.
- understand the concept of constant ratio.

Overview

Teams will measure the circumference of different-sized cookies with string to discover constant ratios of radius, diameter, and x. Cost comparisons using ratios in unit pricing will be introduced.

Time

Two 30–45 minute periods

Team Size

Two to three students

Materials

String; rulers; round cookies in three different sizes, with brand name (or type), cost, and number of cookies in package displayed; fraction calculators or scientific calculators

Procedure

1. Before using this activity, introduce students to the concept of ratio.

2. Have each team select three different cookies to measure.

3. You should specify the unit of measure, inches or centimeters, for each group. If some groups use inches and some use centimeters, it should help reinforce the concept that the ratio is constant, no matter what unit of measure is used.

4. Students will use the string to measure the distance around the cookie and across it. To find the radius, they must estimate where the center of the cookie is and measure to the edge.

5. The first part of the lab should provide hands-on experience of what *circumference* means ("the distance around"). Students should also discover the idea of *constant ratio* in comparing the ratios of circumference to diameter, diameter to radius, and radius to diameter.

6. You may wish to discuss further the concept of π and its relationship to the circumference and diameter. It is important to note, however, that π is an irrational number that cannot be expressed as a fraction. The constant ratio of circumference to diameter is an approximation of π, as is the commonly-used $\frac{22}{7}$.

7. The second part of the lab teaches the concept of ratio as rate by comparing the costs of the cookies.

8. Questions 5 and 6 could be opened up for class discussion. Of particular interest would be the students' creation of ratio problems in question 6.

Circumference of Cookies and Cost Comparison

In this lab, you will compare the distance around different cookies to the distance across. You will need three different cookies, string, and a ruler.

Vocabulary

Circumference: The length around a circle.

Radius: The distance from the center of a circle to the circle's edge.

Diameter: The length of a line segment passing through the center of the circle whose endpoints are on the circle's edge.

Circumference of Cookies

In the following chart, list the brand or type of cookie. With your string, measure the distance around the cookie (circumference), across the cookie (diameter), and from the center of the cookie to the edge (radius). Record your measurements on the chart.

Brand	Circum-ference (c)	Diameter (d)	Radius (r)	$\dfrac{c}{d}$	$\dfrac{d}{r}$	$\dfrac{r}{d}$

1. For each cookie, record on the chart the ratio of the circumference to the diameter (%). What do you notice?

_____

_____

_____

(continued)

Circumference of Cookies
and Cost Comparison (continued)

2. Record on the chart the ratio of the diameter to the radius (%). What do you notice?

_____

_____

_____

_____

_____

3. Record on the chart the ratio of the radius to the diameter (⅟₂). What do you notice?

_____

_____

_____

_____

_____

Cost Comparison

Fill in the following chart.

Brand or type	Cost of package	Number of cookies in package	Cost of 1 cookie (cost ÷ no. of cookies)	Cost of cookie per unit of circumference

(continued)

Circumference of Cookies
and Cost Comparison *(continued)*

1. According to your chart, which cookie is the most expensive per centimeter?

   _____

2. According to your chart, which cookie is the least expensive per centimeter?

   _____

3. Should you buy the brand (or type) in question 2 just because it is the least expensive cookie?

   _____

   _____

4. Name three different considerations you should take into account *besides* the price when making your cookie selection.

   _____

   _____

   _____

5. Discuss the various benefits and uses of ratios in real-life situations.

   _____

   _____

   _____

   _____

6. Create another ratio problem using cookies. Write your problem below.

   _____

   _____

   _____

Pizza, Pizza, Pizza

Learning Outcome

Students will be able to:

- realize the difference between circumference and area.

- discover the effect of changing a diameter on circumference and area.

Overview

Students will experiment with various circles to discover the effect changing diameters have on circumference and area. They will then roll various circles on the floor to measure circumference and trace the same circles on squared grid paper for area.

Time

Two 45–60-minute periods

Team Size

Two to three students

Materials

Cardboard circles with diameters of 2 inches, 3 inches, 4 inches, 6 inches, 8 inches, and 12 inches (one of each size for each group); measuring tools; 40"-long paper; square-inch grid paper; calculators

Procedure

Activity One:

1. Give each team one circle of each size.

2. As students work on the first question, you may wish to observe the responses. Students should realize that the size of pizza is based on diameter, not radius. If confusion arises, a class discussion about radius and diameter may be needed.

3. Next, students will mark a starting point on a piece of plain paper and roll the circle one complete revolution, holding the circle perpendicular to the paper, like a wheel. You may wish to model this. Student then measure the distance to find the circumference for each circle.

4. Students continue this process for the various sizes and record the data on the chart on their lab pages. They should discover that doubling the diameter doubles the circumference.

(continued)

Activity Two

1. The first question usually brings the response that doubling the diameter will double the area.

2. Students trace their 6-inch circle on square grid paper and count the squares contained within for an approximate area. They then do the same thing for the 12-inch circle. They should discover that the area of the 12-inch circle is four times as large as the area of the 6-inch circle.

3. Have the students test further with other circles to verify their discovery.

Activity Three

1. Based on their discoveries above, various responses to the first question are possible. Some may still believe that to double the size, they should double the price. Others may try a proportion approach to determine the prices—that is, the price of a 6-inch relative to its size is equal to the price of a 12-inch relative to its size. You may wish to have each team discuss how they set their prices.

2. The second question reinforces the effect doubling the diameter has on the circumference and area of a circle.

Activity Four

1. This activity may be used as an extension. For homework, assign the task of collecting prices on different size cheese pizzas from various pizza places.

2. During the next class, the students work in their teams, organizing their data on the chart provided and comparing prices. This provides for rich discussion of what factors determine price. Is it just cost, or do packaging, taste, etc., influence the price?

Pizza, Pizza, Pizza

Activity One

Let's pretend that you and your partner(s) want to go into business and open up a pizza shop. You've decided first to investigate selling 6" and 12" cheese pizzas.

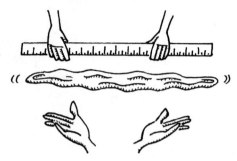

When a customer orders a 6" or 12" pizza, what does the 6" or 12" refer to?

_____

_____

You and your partner(s) will be given cardboard models of 6" and 12" round pizzas. Determine the distance around the 6" pizza by marking a point on the outside edge of the pizza. Next, mark a starting point on a piece of plain paper and roll the circle one complete revolution. Measure this length and record in inches.

Distance around 6" pizza: _____

How do you think the measure of this distance will compare with the distance around the 12" circle?

_____

_____

Measure the distance around the 12" model in the same way and record the length of one revolution. This measurement gives you the circumference, the distance around the circle.

Distance around 12" pizza: _____

When you double the diameter, what happens to the circumference?

_____

_____

Test your discovery three more times by measuring the lengths of one revolution of the following circles and comparing their lengths: 2" and 4" circles, 3" and 6" circles, 4" and 8" circles. Record on the chart on the next page.

(continued)

Pizza, Pizza, Pizza *(continued)*

Circle size	Length of one revolution of circle
2"	
4"	
3"	
6"	
4"	
8"	
6"	
12"	

Do the above data support your previous statement about how doubling the diameter affects the circumference? Restate your discovery here.

_____

_____

_____

_____

Activity Two

Now, let's explore: Will doubling the diameter double the area? What do you think?

_____

_____

_____

(continued)

Pizza, Pizza, Pizza *(continued)*

With your partner(s), trace the circumference of the 3" circle on square-inch grid paper. Approximately how many squares does the 3" circle contain?

_____

Next, trace the circumference of the 6" circle on square-inch grid paper. Approximately how many squares does the 6" circle contain?

_____

Now, compare the estimated total number of squares contained within each circle. Approximately how many times larger is the 6" circle area than the 3" circle area?

_____

Show the math you use to figure this out. You may use your calculator.

What statements can you write about your discovery?

_____

_____

_____

Now test your discovery by comparing the estimated total of squares contained within: 2" and 4" circles. Show the math you use to figure this out. You may use your calculator.

Do the new data prove or disprove your discovery?

_____

_____

_____

(continued)

Pizza, Pizza, Pizza (continued)

Activity Three

You and your partner(s) must determine what size pizzas you will sell in your restaurant and the price you will charge for each. To begin, figure the sizes and prices for cheese pizzas. Some questions to think about are:

1. How will you figure the price of each size of pizza? For example, if you charge $3.50 for a small, round 12" cheese pizza and $4.25 for a medium, round 14" cheese pizza, which is the better buy?

   _____

2. When the circumference of a pizza pan doubles, should you double the price? Explain your reasoning.

   _____

   _____

   _____

   _____

Activity Four

You and your partner(s) have decided to compare prices of cheese pizzas sold at three shops in town. Each of you will get prices for a 12", 14", and 16" cheese pizza at your favorite shop and bring them to the next class. Record this information on the following chart.

Name of Shop	12" Price	14" Price	16" Price

Use these pizza prices to determine the best buys in town for cheese pizzas. Then determine how you will price your cheese pizzas. What factors will affect the price you charge? Brainstorm with your partners and list as many things as you can think of that will affect the price, such as labor cost, price of ingredients, etc.

Volume

Learning Outcomes

Students will be able to:

- work with three-dimensional figures, find volume, and label with correct units.

- apply concepts of volume to real life applications.

Overview

Using strategies of estimation and measurement, students, given a few boxes, will determine how many boxes are needed to fill a truckload.

Time

Two 45–60-minute class periods

Team Size

Three or four students

Materials

Centimeter cubes or unifix cubes; small and medium cardboard boxes of various sizes; rulers; calculators

Procedure

Activity One

1. Give each group enough cubes to build at least five floors (100 to 200 cubes).

2. Through a hands-on application, students should begin to see that volume is found by finding the area of the first floor times the number of floors.

3. The last question asks students to think further about volume. They should realize that volume can also measure the space inside a building.

Activity Two

1. This activity offers student more hands-on applications of volume.

2. Give each group four boxes of different sizes. Students measure the sides of each box, then determine how many cubes are needed to fill each box. The question that usually arises is, what part is the length, width, and height? Through discovery, students should see that the parts are interchangeable—that is, the commutative property of multiplication allows the measures to be rearranged and still give the same volume.

(continued)

Activity Three

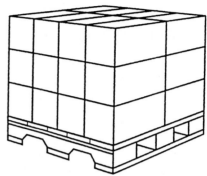

1. This activity connects volume to a real-life application. Give each team one of the boxes used in activity two.

2. Students are given the dimensions of a truck, and are asked to determine how many boxes of the size they have been given will fit on pallets in the truck. For competition purposes, have two teams have identical box A's, two teams box B, etc. Doing this allows students to see if the other team arrives at the same conclusions that they do.

3. When all groups have developed their plans, have them present the plans to the class. This allows them to see various ways to approach the problem.

4. Some students may choose to find the volume of the truck and divide this by the volume of one pallet with boxes stacked on it. This approach does not take into consideration how many pallets will fit on the truck floor. While mathematically it may be sound, realistically, the pallets are limited to 2 across and 11 down in the truck.

Extensions

Students might be encouraged to ask trucking companies how volume is calculated for truck loads, how much it costs to ship something, and how articles are loaded on a pallet.

Volume

Activity One

Using centimeter cubes construct an "apartment building." The first floor of the building should be four cubes by five cubes. Continue construction, making your building five stories tall, then ten stories tall.

How many cubes were needed for the five story building? _____

the ten story building? _____

How would you determine the amount of blocks needed for a building 125 stories high? Explain your method below.

If you built an apartment building using solid cubes, you wouldn't be able to enter the building. What do you think was the purpose for doing the above activity?

_____

_____

_____

_____

Activity Two

Using the four boxes assigned by your teacher, measure the length, width, and height of each to the nearest inch. Then see how many cubes it takes to fill each box. Record in the chart.

(continued)

Volume (continued)

Box	Length	Width	Height	Total of Cubes
Box A				
Box B				
Box C				
Box D				

What similarities do you observe about the four boxes?

_____

_____

_____

_____

Does it matter which side is labeled the length, the width, or the height?

_____

_____

_____

_____

Activity Three

You are a crew member on the loading dock of a trucking company. Your supervisor has given your crew the task of determining how many boxes can be shipped of a particular size. The inside dimensions of the trailer of the truck are Height = 109 inches, Width = 97 inches, and Length = 47 feet.

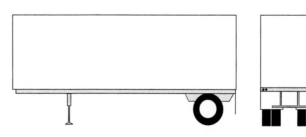

(continued)

Volume (continued)

Your supervisor want your crew to load the boxes on pallets that are 48 inches by 48 inches by 5 inches. The task is to figure how many boxes can fit on a pallet and how many pallets will fit inside the trailer.

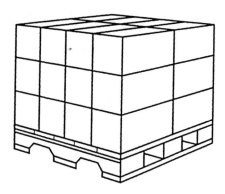

Each of the eight crews are assigned the task of determining how many boxes of one size can be shipped in a trailer. Since there are four boxes of different sizes, your crew will be assigned the same box as another crew and will compete for the best way to ship the most boxes in the trailer.

Working Plan

I am a member of team _____ and we have been assigned box _____ to ship. The following represents our plan and calculations to be presented to you, our supervisor, and the rest of the crews.

_____

_____

_____

_____

_____

_____

_____

_____

_____

_____

_____

The Largest Cylinder Is . . .

Learning Outcomes

Students will be able to:

- understand the differences among perimeter, area, and volume.
- estimate capacity of a cylindrical object.
- calculate using the volume formula.

Overview

Students construct two cylinders using the same sized paper and determine, by estimation, if the volumes are equal or not. By filling their cylinders with rice, the students will prove if their guess was correct.

Time

45–60 minutes

Team Size

Three or four students

Materials

8½"×11" construction paper or oaktag (five sheets per group); rulers; tape; rice; measuring cups; cartons to contain cylinders as they are being filled

Procedure

1. You may wish to begin by reviewing the concepts of perimeter and area of a rectangle, and the formulas for finding the perimeter and area.

2. Distribute five sheets of construction paper or oaktag to each group. Model the process of making both a tall cylinder and a short one. Then have students proceed to make their own cylinders.

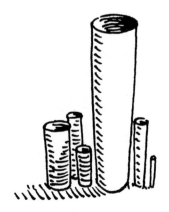

(continued)

3. As students construct their cylinders, some may butt the edges of the paper, while others overlap the sides, then tape. If students ask you which way is "correct," suggest they try both approaches to see if they get the same results with both approaches, or if the results are different.

4. Once students have made both a short and a tall cylinder, they should stand both cylinders upright and guess which one will hold more rice. It is not necessary for all group members to agree on an estimate. Most students usually guess that the 11" cylinder will have a greater capacity than the 8½" one, and are surprised to find that the opposite is true.

5. One at a time, students should place the cylinders inside a carton (to keep the rice in one place) and fill the cylinder with rice, then measure the amount of rice each cylinder held and record the amount on the lab sheet.

6. If students did not overlap the edges of their sheets of paper, then using the formula for volume of a cylinder will give the following results:

Cylinder A (h = 11 inches)	Cylinder B (h = 8.5 inches)
Diameter = 2.7 inches	Diameter = 3.5 inches
Radius = 1.35 inches	Radius = 1.75 inches
Volume = $\pi r^2 h$	Volume = $\pi r^2 h$
$V = \pi (1.35)^2 11$	$V = \pi (1.75)^2 8.5$
$V = 3.14 \cdot 1.82 \cdot 11$	$V = 3.14 \cdot 3.06 \cdot 8.5$
$V = 62.94$ cubic inches	$V = 81.67$ cubic inches

7. Have groups test their discovery by building more cylinders of different sizes and reporting their findings. You may want to create a class data chart to record findings.

8. Once students have responded to the questions on their lab sheets, have groups share their thoughts for a class discussion.

Extension

Have students examine grocery store products packaged in different cylinders. What kinds of products use cylinders? What types of cylinders? Why?

The Largest Cylinder Is . . .

1. With your partner take an 8½" by 11" piece of paper. Find the perimeter and then the area of the paper. Show the formula for each and your work below.

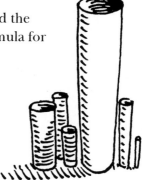

2. Your next task is to form two different cylinders from the same size piece of paper. First take an 8½" by 11" piece of paper, roll it lengthwise into a cylinder, and tape the edges. Second, take the same size paper but roll it widthwise into a cylinder and tape the edges. You should have two cylinders, one whose height is 11" and one whose height is 8½". Draw sketches of your cylinders here. Label the height *h* and the base *b* on each cylinder.

3. Observe each cylinder. **Make a guess** as to which cylinder will hold the most rice. Is it the cylinder whose height is 11" or the cylinder whose height is 8½"? Or are the two volumes equal?

I think _____

because _____

_____

(continued)

The Largest Cylinder Is . . . *(continued)*

4. One at a time, stand your cylinders in a carton. Fill each cylinder with rice. Record the amount of rice each one holds here.

    11" cylinder: _____

    8½" cylinder: _____

    Was your guess about volume correct? _____

5. Now use your ruler to measure the diameter of each cylinder. Then determine the radius of each one.

    Cylinder A (h = 11 inches)   Cylinder B (h = 8.5 inches)

    Diameter: _____   Diameter: _____

    Radius: _____   Radius: _____

6. The formula for the volume of a cylinder is:

    $$\text{Volume} = \pi\, r^2\, h$$

    Use this formula to find the volume of both your cylinders. Use your calculator to help you with the computations.

    Cylinder A (h = 11 inches)   Cylinder B (h = 8.5 inches)

    Volume: _____   Volume: _____

7. Do the experiment again, using a different-sized piece of paper for both cylinders. Between you, you should now have three sets of data. Write your observations below.

    _____

    _____

    _____

    _____

    _____

    _____

(continued)

The Largest Cylinder Is . . . *(continued)*

8. What conclusions can you draw from this activity?

_____

_____

_____

9. How might manufacturers use this information?

_____

_____

_____

10. Do you think most consumers think tall containers always give you more?

_____

_____

11. Knowing what you know now, if you were going to sell a new product in a cylinder, what kind of cylinder would you want your product in?

_____

_____

Angle Measure

Learning Outcome

Students will be able to:

- label and measure angles of a triangle, rectangle, and irregular quadrilateral.

- discover that the sum of the angles of a triangle is 180° and the sum of the angles of a quadrilateral is 360.°

Overview

In this activity students trace a triangle, a rectangle, and an irregularly-shaped quadrilateral. By measuring the angles, students discover some angle properties for triangles and quadrilaterals.

Time

45–60 minutes

Team Size

Two students

Materials

Cardboard cutouts of one triangle, one rectangle, one irregular quadrilateral*; paper; protractors

*Make sure that the cut-out shapes are different sizes for the different groups. If you use the template on page 89, enlarge it at different proportions for each group.

The lab assumes that students have had prior experience measuring angles with a protractor. You may want to review measuring with a protractor or teach this skill prior to beginning the lab.

1. Each team traces around each shape, then labels the angles in each shape.

2. Watch how and where students label their angles (see Figures 1 and 2). They should label inside the vertex, not along a side.

3. Many students have trouble measuring the angles in shapes because they have difficulty seeing the sides that form the angle. If this is the case, suggest that students trace the angle with their fingers or cover up the edges that do not make the angle.

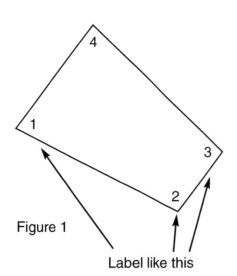

Figure 1

Label like this

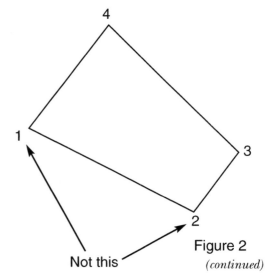

Not this

Figure 2
(continued)

70

4. Also watch how students measure using the protractor. Some may read the wrong scale. You may need to review the terms acute and obtuse and how to read the protractor correctly.

5. When groups have finished measuring their angles, create a master chart on the board or overhead. Record each group's findings on the master chart. Discoveries made should be the following:

   • The total measure of the angles of a triangle is 180°, regardless of the shape or size of the triangle.

   • The total measure of the angles of any quadrilateral, not just rectangles, is 360°, regardless of shape or size.

Angle Measure

With your partner, take three cardboard shapes: a triangle, a rectangle, and a four-sided irregular shape.

1. Trace your three shapes on a separate piece of paper.

2. Label the angles.

3. Then measure the angles within each shape using your protractor.

4. Have your partner check your measurements as you double-check your partner's.

5. Record your measurements on the chart on the next page.

6. Enter your measurements on the teacher's class chart.

After all teams have recorded their data on the class chart, brainstorm with your partner about what you observe. Write your observations below. Be ready to share your thoughts with the class.

_____

_____

_____

_____

_____

_____

_____

_____

_____

(continued)

Angle Measure (continued)

Shape	Angle Measure in Degrees
Triangle	
<1	_____
<2	_____
<3	_____
	Total Degrees _____
Rectangle	
<1	_____
<2	_____
<3	_____
<4	_____
	Total Degrees _____
Four-Sided Irregular Shape	
<1	_____
<2	_____
<3	_____
<4	_____
	Total Degrees _____

The Most Common Words in English

Learning Outcome

Students will be able to:

- understand word frequency and its relationship to mathematics.
- reinforce ratios as percents using various methods.
- reinforce proportions.

Overview

Student teams are given three news articles (national, sports, and local) to read, summarize, and determine the frequency of the 25 most common words in English, which comprise one third of all printed material.

Time

Two 30–45-minute periods

Team Size

Three students

Materials

Newspapers, or various articles clipped from newspapers; calculators

Procedure

1. Before beginning the activity, you may want to discuss the meaning and use of the word *frequency*.

2. To save time, assign reading the articles and writing the summaries as homework activities. Each student could prepare one article, and the team members could then share summaries with each other.

3. Allow students to change ratios to percents using various methods. Reinforce their methods by explaining them in the lab.

4. Create a class chart of the words and their frequencies on the board or overhead. Record each group's findings on the chart.

5. After all data are logged on the class chart, ask students to share their methods of computing percents and their answers to question 7.

Extensions

- Have students prove from their findings and the data of their classmates that these 25 words (a) are the most common words in English, (b) are ranked in order of frequency, and (c) make up about one-third of all printed material. Reinforce that these words are listed in terms of frequency and that the total list makes up about $\frac{1}{3}$ or $33\frac{1}{3}$ percent of all written words. Give students ample time to work on this; then have students share their findings with the class. Hopefully, students will use a variety of mathematical concepts including fraction and ratio knowledge, averaging, and proportions.

- Encourage students to determine the word frequencies in creative stories that they have written to see if the frequency holds true for fiction as well as nonfiction.

The Most Common Words in English

"One third of all printed material in English is made up of 25 common words." Do you believe this statement is true? With your partners, select three articles from your local newspaper: a front-page world or national article, a sports article, and a local article.

   Read and summarize each article. Count the total number of words and then the frequency of each word listed on the chart on page 78. Record your numbers on the chart.

Article 1: Front Page

The name of our article: _____

_____

A brief summary of our article: _____

_____

_____

_____

_____

_____

_____

_____

_____

_____

The total number of words in article 1: _____

(continued)

The Most Common Words in English *(continued)*

Article 2: Sports Page

The title of our article: _____

_____

A brief summary of our article: _____

_____

_____

_____

_____

_____

_____

_____

_____

_____

_____

_____

_____

_____

The total number of words in article 2: _____

(continued)

The Most Common Words in English *(continued)*

Article 3: Local Page

The title of our article: _____

_____

A brief summary of our article: _____

_____

_____

_____

_____

_____

_____

_____

_____

_____

_____

_____

_____

_____

The total number of words in article 3: _____

(continued)

77   *Math for All Learners: Pre-Algebra*

The Most Common Words in English *(continued)*

Now compare the frequencies of words occurring in each article by filling in the frequency columns in the following chart. (Remember, frequency is the number of times a word appears in an article divided by the total number of words in the article.) Next, convert the frequency to a percent. On the back of this page, explain how you did this. Total the percent column for each article.

Words	Front Page		Sports Page		Local Page	
	Freq.	Percent	Freq.	Percent	Freq.	Percent
1. the						
2. of						
3. and						
4. a						
5. to						
6. in						
7. is						
8. you						
9. that						
10. it						
11. he						
12. was						
13. for						
14. on						
15. are						
16. as						
17. with						
18. his						
19. they						
20. I						
21. at						
22. be						
23. this						
24. have						
25. from						
	Total:		Total:		Total:	

(continued)

The Most Common Words in English (continued)

Now analyze your data from the chart and answer the following questions:

1. Which word appeared **the most** in the front-page article? _____

   in the sports article? _____

   in the local article? _____

2. Does this word represent the same percent in each article?

   _____

3. Which word appeared **the least** in the front-page article? _____

   in the sports article? _____

   in the local article? _____

4. Does this word represent the same percent in each article?

   _____

5. Do you have other words that represent an equal ratio or percent in all three articles?

   _____

6. If you answered no to question 5, is there a word that was at the same ratio for two out of the three articles?

   _____

7. These words make up about one third, or 33⅓ percent, of all printed material in English. Look at your total percents for the three articles. Are your results close to 33⅓ percent? _____

8. Record your findings on the class data chart. Be ready to answer the following questions in a class discussion.

   a. Which word occurred the most over all?

   b. Which word occurred the least over all?

   c. Were there any frequency variations among your classmates? If so, how do you explain this?

   d. How does the number of samples affect the data?

   e. Do you think there is a better mathematical way to determine more accurate frequencies?

m&m's™ and Math

Learning Outcome

Students will be able to:

- recognize a ratio (a comparison of two numbers by division).

- express a ratio as a fraction, decimal, and percent.

- understand the statistical terms **mean** and **median**.

- use data from a chart to calculate a mean and a median.

Overview

Students will use m&m's to find ratio, percent, mean, and median of the various colors, and will compare individual data to class data.

Time

Two 45–60-minute periods

Team Size

Three to four students

Materials

Bags of m&m's for each student (1.69 oz. or 47.9 g size or larger); paper towels to put m&m's on; calculators; 9" paper plate

Procedure

Activity One

1. Caution students not to eat the m&m's until they have finished steps 1 and 2 of Activity One.

2. If students have no prior knowledge of percents, don't teach them but use the lab as a starting point to see what they know about percents. Their knowledge will become evident when you ask them to estimate the percent of each color from their ratios and then write their strategies for making these estimations.

3. If you feel students need direct teaching on how to calculate the actual percent, model step 6 of the lab. This lab can reinforce fractions, decimals, and percent equivalents, or it can be an introduction to the concepts.

4. After all groups have calculated their percents of each color, create a class data chart on an overhead or the blackboard, similar to the chart on page 85. Have students record their individual data on the chart, then study all the data.

(continued)

5. Discuss each team's observations. Ask why some students got a total of 100 percent while others computed over or under 100 percent for their totals. On the overhead or blackboard, list their reasons for these discrepancies. The main reason is that rounding each percent can sometimes make the total seem greater or less than 100 percent. If students carried their percents out to two or more decimal places, the margin of error would be minimal.

Activity Two

1. If students have never been introduced to the statistical terms of **mean** and **median**, teach a mini-lesson before students engage in the activity.

2. Students' ages, temperatures, and basketball scores are good examples to show mean and median. Regardless of the data you choose to use for modeling, place the data on the board randomly. Discuss **mean** first, as many students probably have been introduced to the concept of the average or heard of the average temperature for a particular time span or the average score or grade, etc. Ask students to discuss with their teams examples of where they have heard the word **average** used. Then have them write their thoughts on their lab sheet and discuss them with the whole class.

3. Take one of their most frequent ideas and have students help you make up sample data to demonstrate how you calculate the mean, which is nothing more than the average. Tell them they must find the total of their data and then divide by the number of data entries represented. Allow use of the calculator.

   Example: Average high temperature for the week of July 4 in Florida is calculated by taking the week's daily highs (89, 93, 95, 88, 94, 96, 92), finding the total, and dividing by 7 (days).

4. After you model two or three examples, have students return to their teams to see if they can determine the generalization or formula for calculating any mean problem. The following is the algebraic formula, but many responses will be given, depending on the math skills of the students.

$$\frac{x_1 + x_2 + x_3 + \ldots + x_n}{n} = m$$

5. Next, use the temperature data used to model the mean to introduce the median. See first if any student knows or has heard the word **median**. Tell students the data must be listed in a special way, from smallest to largest numerical value, to calculate the median. While modeling, tell students that in a list containing an odd number of data, the median is always the middle number, but for an even number of numbers, the median is the average of the two middle numbers.

6. Using the sample data generated from the class for the mean, have students calculate the median and compare the two. Have them discuss with their teams what they notice about the mean and the median.

(continued)

7. Now students have a foundation for calculating the mean and the median in activity 2 using their m&m's data.

8. Have students work in their teams to calculate the mean and median.

9. After students read the statistic on the percentages of each color that should be in their bags, have them answer the questions.

Extensions

• In a 16 oz. bag of m&m's, there are approximately 500 candies. About how many of each color would be in the bag? (brown—150; yellow—100; red—100; green—100; orange—50)

• Calculate the weight of each m&m in a 16 ounce bag with approximately 500 candies in it.

$$(\frac{16}{500} = .032 \text{ ounces})$$

• According to the information on the bag, one serving is about 1.5 oz. How many servings would be in a pound package?

$$(\frac{16}{1.5} = 10.6\bar{6} \text{ servings})$$

How many pieces in each serving?

$$(\frac{.032}{1 \text{ m\&m's}} = \frac{1.5}{? \text{ m\&m's}} \text{ or } \frac{1.5}{.032} = 46.875 = 47 \text{ m\&m's})$$

• If there are 240 calories in one serving of m&m's, about how many calories does each m&m contain?

$$(\frac{240}{46.875} = \frac{?}{1} = 5.12 \text{ calories in each m\&m})$$

m&m's™ and Math

Activity One

1. Open your bag of m&m's and organize them in some way. Please **do not eat any** until you have finished the lab. Share with your partners how you organized your m&m's. Write what you observe about the contents of your bag.

   _____

   _____

2. Count the m&m's in your bag. Total m&m's: _____
   How many of each color are represented in your bag? Record the totals below.

   Green _____   **Orange** _____   **Red** _____

   Blue _____   **Yellow** _____   **Brown** _____

3. What ratio does each color represent? A ratio is a comparison of two numbers to show a relationship. The ratio of each color would be

   $$\frac{\textbf{number of each color}}{\textbf{total in bag}}$$

   Write the ratio for each color below.

   Green _____   **Orange** _____   **Red** _____

   Blue _____   **Yellow** _____   **Brown** _____

4. Place a paper plate upside down on your table or desk. Arrange your m&m's by color around the circumference of the plate. Make a complete circle. The complete circle represents one whole, or 100%, so:

   half the circle represents _____%

   one quarter of the circle represents _____%

(continued)

m&m's™ and Math (continued)

5. Using your circle of m&m's as a visual aid, estimate the percent of each color.

   Green _____ **Orange** _____ **Red** _____

   Blue _____ **Yellow** _____ **Brown** _____

6. Please explain how you estimated the percent each color of m&m represented in your bag. Discuss your strategies with your partners. Write your explanation for the most reasonable strategy.

   _____

   _____

   _____

   _____

   _____

7. Do you know how to calculate the actual percent of each color found in your bag? _____ If so, calculate the actual percents and record them. If not, here's how: Use your calculator to divide the number of each color by the total number in the bag. Multiply your answer by 100 to get the percent.

   $$\frac{\textbf{total of one color m\&m}}{\textbf{total m\&m's}} \times 100 = \text{_____}\%$$

   Green _____ **Orange** _____ **Red** _____

   Blue _____ **Yellow** _____ **Brown** _____

   Add together the percents for all the colors to get the total percent. Write it here.

   _____

(continued)

m&m's™ and Math (continued)

8. Post your results on the class data chart. Log all the data on the chart below, and total the results.

m & m Class Data Chart

Name	Percent Green	Percent Orange	Percent Red	Percent Blue	Percent Yellow	Percent Brown

(continued)

m&m's™ and Math (continued)

9. After examining the class data, what observations can you make?

_____

_____

_____

_____

Activity Two

1. Discuss with your partners real-life situations in which you have heard the word **average** used. List them below. Be ready to discuss your thoughts with the entire class.

_____

_____

_____

2. After you and your class have discussed real-life situations, make up sample data to fit the situations mentioned. Record the data below, then compute the average for each.

Situation #1	Situation #2	Situation #3
_____	_____	_____
Average	Average	Average

(continued)

m&m's™ and Math *(continued)*

3. Write a generalization or way to determine the average (also called the **mean**) for any given situation. Discuss it with your partners and be ready to share with the class.

_____

_____

_____

4. Now discuss the word **median**. Have you or anyone in your group heard this word used? What do you think it means?

_____

_____

_____

5. After your teacher explains and models the median for you, use the data from step 2 to determine the median for each set of data. Calculate below.

6. Can you and your team draw any conclusions about the mean and median based on your calculations? If so, what are they?

_____

_____

_____

(continued)

m&m's™ and Math *(continued)*

7. Using the data from the m&m's chart, calculate the mean and median percent for each color.

Mean %

Green _____ **Orange** _____ **Red** _____

Blue _____ **Yellow** _____ **Brown** _____

Median %

Green _____ **Orange** _____ **Red** _____

Blue _____ **Yellow** _____ **Brown** _____

8. According to statistics, if you examine many bags of m&m's, you will find that about **30** percent of the candies are brown, **20** percent yellow, **20** percent red, **10** percent green, **10** percent blue, and **10** percent orange.

   a. Which figure—the mean or the median—do you think was used to calculate the above statistics? Please explain.

   _____

   _____

   b. How did your bag of m&m's compare with these data?

   _____

   _____

   c. What conclusions can you draw from this activity?

   _____

   _____

Geometric Shapes Template

1-Centimeter Grid

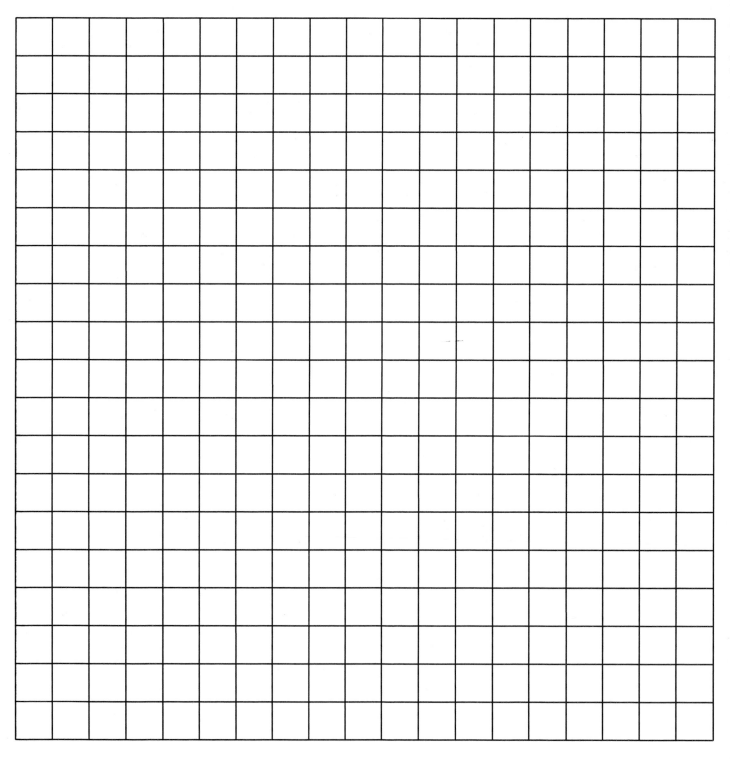